ideals®

FRIENDSHIP ISSUE

Connie Score

Lord, we thank Thee
for this place in which we dwell;
for the love
that unites us;
for the peace accorded us this day;
for the hope with which we expect the morrow; for the health,
the work, the food, and the bright skies
that make our lives delightful; for our friends in all parts of the earth.
Give us courage, gaiety, and the quiet mind.
Spare to us our friends; soften to us our enemies.
Bless us, if it may be, in all our innocent endeavors.
If it may not, give us the strength to encounter that
which is to come, that we may be brave in peril, constant in tribulation,
temperate in wrath and in all changes of fortune and,
down to the gates of death, loyal and loving one to another.

Robert Louis Stevenson

Editorial Director, James Kuse
Managing Editor, Ralph Luedtke
Associate Editor, Colleen Callahan Gonring
Production Editor/Manager, Richard Lawson
Photographic Editor, Gerald Koser

Winter in the Country

The country in winter's a beautiful sight
When the sky is so blue o'er a field of white.
There's a farm nestled down below the hill
And the countryside's wrapped in a quiet chill.

The wonders of winter are free to all,
The frozen cascade of a waterfall,
A shawl for the hedgerows, an icicle crown
On the farmhouse roof where the snow melted down.

The firs and the pines bending down with snow,
And tracks o'er the meadow of buck and doe,
A colorful streak of a bird in flight,
The gleam on the snow when the sun sets bright.

The country in winter's a sight to behold,
Farmland coverlet-draped icy and cold.
There's wonder and beauty wherever you go
When the countryside's wrapped in a new-fallen snow.

Mildred L. Jarrell

ISBN 0-89542-318-9   295

IDEALS—Vol. 36 No. 1, January 1979. IDEALS is published eight times a year, January, February, March, May, July, September, November and December—
by IDEALS PUBLISHING CORPORATION, 11315 Watertown Plank Road, Milwaukee, Wis. 53226.
Second-class postage paid at Milwaukee, Wisconsin. Copyright © 1978 by IDEALS PUBLISHING CORPORATION.
All rights reserved. Title IDEALS registered U.S. Patent Office.

ONE YEAR SUBSCRIPTION—eight consecutive issues as published—only $16.00
TWO YEAR SUBSCRIPTION—sixteen consecutive issues as published—only $28.00
SINGLE ISSUES—only $2.95

Photograph opposite
Robert Holland

Home, Sweet Home

An exile from home, splendor dazzles in vain;
Oh, give me my lowly thatched cottage again!
The birds singing gaily, that came at my call—
Give me them—and the peace of mind, dearer than all!
Home, home, sweet, sweet home!
There's no place like home,
    oh, there's no place like home!

Mid pleasures and palaces though we may roam,
Be it ever so humble, there's no place like home;
A charm from the sky seems to hallow us there,
Which, seek through the world, is ne'er met with elsewhere.
Home, home, sweet, sweet home!
There's no place like home,
    oh, there's no place like home!

I gaze on the moon as I tread the drear wild,
And feel that my mother now thinks of her child
As she looks on that moon from our own cottage door
Thro' the woodbine, whose fragrance shall cheer me no more.
Home, home, sweet, sweet home!
There's no place like home,
    oh, there's no place like home!

How sweet 'tis to sit neath a fond father's smile,
And the caress of a mother to soothe and beguile!
Let others delight mid new pleasures to roam,
But give me, oh, give me, the pleasures of home.
Home, home, sweet, sweet home!
There's no place like home,
    oh, there's no place like home!

To thee I'll return, overburdened with care;
The heart's dearest solace will smile on me there;
No more from that cottage again will I roam;
Be it ever so humble, there's no place like home.
Home, home, sweet, sweet home!
There's no place like home,
    oh, there's no place like home!

John Howard Payne

Winter Coverlets

Mildred L. Jarrell

Winter spins her coverlets,
Soft as eiderdown,
From gently falling flakes of white
And lays them all around,

Winter weaves her frosty lace
To cover brooks and streams,
Fairy stitching to the banks
With frilly, crystal seams.

Winter drapes an ermine cloak
O'er mighty mountains high,
And knits an icy stocking cap
On peaks that reach the sky.

Wraps the sleeping earth beneath
In comforters so light,
Tucks the hills and valleys in
From bleak and bitter night.

Winter's soft, white arms embrace
The barren earth below,
And shelter her with cozy quilts
All made of fluffy snow.

Mountaintops

Ruth H. Underhill

Towering giants high above
Peering to earth below,
Rugged purple mountaintops
Capped with shimmering snow.

Strong and stately mountains
Standing firmly in their place
Staunchly show their majesty
On a proud and regal face.

Reaching, reaching ever upward
Into the heavens on high
Creating a new and lofty world
Touched by the azure sky.

*Photograph opposite
Wyoming, view of Teton Range
from Snake River Overlook
Russell Lamb*

James J. Metcalfe

For many years, James J. Metcalfe brought encouragement into American homes with his poetic expressions of the little, special episodes of everyday living. His verse appeared daily in a widely syndicated newspaper column and he has published several collections of poetry from that column. Metcalfe, a deeply religious family man, viewed his poetic ability as a gift from God to bring joy and inspiration to his fellowman. His poems about friendship, love and family are his most popular, often inspired by his wife Lillian and their three children. Born in Berlin, Germany, in 1906, he interspersed his colorful journalistic career with brief periods as a lawyer and investigator with the Federal Bureau of Investigaion and the United States Department of Agriculture. On these two pages are a few examples of the many appealing poems that won him admirers around the world.

The Friendly Touch

There is no feeling in this life . . . That I enjoy so much . . . As just to shake the hand of one . . . Who has that friendly touch . . . The one who smiles and says hello . . . Wherever we may meet . . . In happiness or sorrow and . . . In glory or defeat . . . Who is not ever jealous of . . . Another person's gain . . . And does not try to run and hide . . . Each time it looks like rain . . . There is no greater comfort and . . . No more enduring theme . . . Than just to know that someone else . . . Rejoices in my dream . . . That someone wishes me the best . . . Of health and wealth and such . . . And in so many other ways . . . Displays that friendly touch.

Faithful Friend

One all-important part of life . . . Is that of being true . . . In every way to everyone . . . Who is a friend to you . . . To show appreciation by . . . Returning kindly deeds . . . And being quite concerned about . . . The other person's needs . . . By being honest and sincere . . . Dependable and fair . . . And thereby letting it be known . . . How much you really care . . . Because the path of friendship is . . . A path that never bends . . . A path that does not rise or fall . . . And one that never ends . . . And whether joy or tragedy . . . Is knocking on the door . . . The friendship that is faithful will . . . Endure for evermore.

I Thank My Friends

I thank the many friends I have . . . For all they do for me . . . With their encouragement and with . . . Their faithful company . . . They sympathize when I am sad . . . They lift me when I fall . . . And they are always at my side . . . To heed my beck and call . . . Indeed they are the truest friends . . . That anyone could find . . . And that is why their faces are . . . Forever in my mind . . . And that is why their special names . . . Are ever in my heart . . . And why I treasure them and hope . . . That we shall never part . . . I thank my friends eternally . . . Who are so good and true . . . And hope that I may serve them with . . . The deeds I try to do.

Friendly World

The world is such a friendly place . . . In which to spend my time . . . That I am never bothered by . . . The scenery or clime . . . I know that everywhere I go . . . I merely look around . . . And happily another friend . . . Is somewhere to be found . . . A friend I have not met before . . . And do not call by name . . . But who is understanding and . . . Is helpful just the same . . . A friend who has not heard of me . . . And yet who is at hand . . . As real as any neighbor in . . . The most familiar land . . . And so no matter where I go . . . I do not mind the place . . . Because I know that I shall find . . . Another friendly face.

Real Folks

The kind of folks I like to meet . . . Are those whose hearts are gay . . . And who become your friends before . . . The passing of a day . . . You get together and you talk . . . And afterwhile it seems . . . That you have known them all your life . . . If only in your dreams . . . Perhaps you dine with them or have . . . A cup of tea or two . . . Or maybe you just sit around . . . And see the evening through . . . But all of you have put away . . . The cloak that strangers wear . . . And there are pleasant moments of . . . Companionship to share . . . Your hearts are drawn together in . . . The meaning of a smile . . . And you have found the friendliness . . . That makes this life worthwhile.

Capture a Moment

Alice Leedy Mason

Fashion a memory,
    A bright winter scene.
Start with new snow
    Fresh fallen and clean.
Frost-up the windows,
    Fern castles look nice,
Cover the pond
    With a layer of ice.
Wrap all the children
    In fleecy-lined suits,
Knit them some mittens—
    Help with their boots.
Walk proudly down
    To city hall square,

Find a snug shelter
    From sharp frigid air.
Build a warm fire
    That sparkles and glows.
Dry the wet mittens,
    Warm the red nose.
Join in their laughter—
    Welcome their friends.
Sing jolly songs
    Before the fun ends.
Give them, in childhood,
    Good times set apart.
Capture a moment
    To hold in the heart.

On a rare, quiet May morning in 1652 near Lancashire, England, George Fox stood on top of Pendle Hill overlooking the many small towns and villages he had traveled for seven years on a restless, expectant search for the truth—truth as spiritual reality, verified only by inward experience. Fox knew that finding truth meant a sincere conviction "to be faithful to all things, and to act faithfully in two ways—inwardly to God and outwardly to man." From his lofty vantage, Fox experienced a spiritual revelation and "was moved to sound the day of the Lord," envisioning the gathering of a great society of religious friends. Fox finally had developed the confidence to prophesy his divine message of truth—a message that would quickly become the principal theme of Quakerism and the Society of Friends.

The time was right for Fox's vision. The state and Church of England had just experienced a tense period of revolution. Cromwell's Commonwealth army was largely made up of Puritans who, impatient with the Elizabethan reformation, were determined to purify the church of its ceremonies and unscriptural ideas. The Anglican and Puritan churches lost their prestige and authority and the people of England gradually abandoned these established forms of religion, showing an eagerness to support the new movements which had begun to develop— Presbyterians, Baptists, and Independents. At the time, these movements were not established sects and among them were Seekers; thousands of men and women who, like Fox, were searching for spiritual truth and a way of life and worship that would fully express their needs. It was from these Seekers that Fox found the readiest response and greatest support for his message of truth and Society of Friends.

Fox expressed his message of truth across the countryside and hundreds recognized and acknowledged him as the leader for whom they had waited. He spoke in churches and from hillsides, convincing many Seekers of his truth. Fox traveled with and stayed among Seekers who opened their homes and hearts to their new leader. It was during this period that he met Margaret Fell, William Dewsbury, Thomas Aldam and several other influential friends, who would devote their entire lives to helping him convey the message and build the Quakers into a society. The Seekers were continually persecuted by the state, but it was their total commitment to the giving of service and the sharing of friendship and suffering that enabled the Society to endure.

There were no sacraments, sermons, elaborate buildings or paid priests, for they were unnecessary to the Quaker. The truth came from within, so any convenient home was ideal for worship. With each new follower, Fox preached his message of truth with renewed vigor. Those who accepted it and found fellowship within one another's society were friends of truth. Hundreds enthusiastically declared their loyalty and support. The Seekers became founders and the Society of Friends was born.

Only four years after Fox climbed Pendle Hill, his followers were carrying his message to the New World. The society landed in Rhode Island in 1656 and immediately began its fascinating role in America's growth and development. The persecution they had faced in England followed them to the new land. Their books were burned in Boston and Quakers were hanged for maintaining the belief, unlike that of the Massachusetts Puritans, that a church and clergy were not necessary to come into communion with God. These actions provoked William Penn to establish Pennsylvania as a refuge, not only for Quakers, but for all persecuted Christian friends, and Fox's vision of a great society of religious friends had been realized.

A Nodding Acquaintance

A. J. Stich

Where in the world can you find an elegant, Victorian lady seated at a grand piano, a sage Chinese holding his book of wisdom, a courtly gentleman looking very astute, an enchanting black child playing on a bale of cotton and an adorable child tugging hopelessly at her socks —all zestfully nodding with approval? The answer is in a collection of nodders.

You see, a nodder is a delightful figurine with a small pin through the neck. The head is weighted, so a slight touch brings the figure alive with balanced motion lasting for several minutes. Some nodders also have hands and tongues that move.

Nodders are fashioned from bisque, porcelain, jade, wood, teak or ebony and are constructed with artistic precision and refinement. The curious characters come in all sizes and forms, ranging from the prim and stately to the whimsical. Depending on their origin, nodders are lavishly embellished with jewels, precious stones or very rich colors.

These charming characters date before the turn of the century. They fascinated their owners then just as they do admirers and collectors today. Many a Victorian home had a mantel or a special table where nodders were prominently displayed. One nodder that Emperor Maximillian gave his Empress Carlotta in 1864 rests today in the stately living room of their palace in Mexico. A magnificent oriental woman about four feet high is encased in a glass cabinet at the Borromeo Palace at Stresa, Italy. Another exquisite example, inlaid with mother-of-pearl, is in the Royal Palace in Stockholm, Sweden. An extravagant jadeite nodder of the Victorian

*Photographs
A. J. Stich*

era, encrusted with precious jewels, sold for $50,000 at an auction in New York in 1969.

Nodders are sometimes called "pagods" because they are believed to have originated in the Far East where they were used in Chinese temples and shrines. In the eighteenth century, as trade with the Orient became common, the ships of England and Holland returned home with tea, spices and fine porcelains, including nodders. The Europeans were not able to make porcelain until the late eighteenth century when J. F. Bottger discovered the secret at Meissen, Germany. The Meissen Porcelain Works started production, guarding well the secret process for which the kings of Europe had ardently searched.

Meissen was probably the first European company to produce Oriental-style nodders in quantity. Figurines were mass-produced and then sent to the Far East for detailed decoration. Later, they changed to a style of character more familiar to their own people, but several elements common to Oriental nodders were retained. These nodders were often made of glazed, white china, trimmed in cobalt blue, embellished with gold, thus imitating the popular Chinese "Blue Nankin" technique. The handsome figurines became popular in England and it is probable that the British changed the name from pagods to nodders.

Many Oriental nodders hold spread or folded fans. Fans were very popular in England during the eighteenth and nineteenth centuries, and this popularity is reflected in the nodders of that period. The Victorian lady coquettishly used her fan to mystify her lover. Thus many artists incorporated the fan into their nodders, giving their characters an aura of mystique.

The Chelsea, Derby and Bow factories of England produced porcelain nodders for royalty and the elite London society in the period before 1755. They made nodders in the stiff and formal court style of dress. The popular Chinese glazing and decorating techniques were retained and improved. Nodders made in the Chelsea factory can be distinguished by a small, identifying raised anchor. Most nodders have no identifying marks, making it difficult to trace the originating factory.

France made many nodders in both bisque and glazed china, often decorated with delicate colors. The stunning hard-paste bisque nodders of frail ladies and courtly gentlemen created in Chantilly, France, are carefully decorated in subtle pinks, purples and rich golds.

English Staffordshire figures after 1850 were not created to imitate the earlier porcelain nodders. These figures were designed in pottery or earthenware and were produced in large quantities. The Staffordshire clay is often whiter and the parts are molded, not handmade like the earlier nodders. Mass production and molded construction enabled these nodders to be very reasonably priced. The enchanting figures, at one time largely reserved for the aristocracy, could be found in many Victorian homes, usually dressed in quaint costumes with bonnets or hats. An umbrella is often a part of their fashionable attire, since at one time the umbrella was an emblem of royalty in England and the Far East. Some nodders even wore glasses and carried small pets in their arms. Many Staffordshire nodders are found in the United States today.

As the industrialization of Europe took place in the latter part of the nineteenth century, a time of rapid change and confusion ensued. Artisan production was overthrown, forcing a class of talented craftsmen to emerge and immigrate to America. The craftsmen joined their countrymen at various settlements in New England and numerous styles—the Renaissance, the Gothic, baroque and Chinese were revived, and the production of nodders in the United States began.

Today, in a society fascinated by accumulating antiques and artifacts, these intriguing little characters are rapidly becoming a very collectible commodity. Choice examples are being discovered in antique shows, are occasionally advertised in trade magazines and are listed in price guides at auctions. The revival of interest doesn't bother the nodders—they just continue to nod with contented approval.

Enjoy Life

Artur Rubinstein

Famed pianist Artur Rubinstein finds fulfillment in sharing his talent with others. To him the essence of life is doing something truly important to benefit humanity.

I live by one principle: Enjoy life with no conditions! People say, "If I had your health, if I had your money, oh, I would enjoy myself." It is not true. I would be happy if I were lying sick in a hospital bed. It must come from the inside. That is the one thing I hope I have contributed to my children, by example and by talk: to make no conditions, to understand that life is a wonderful thing and to enjoy it, every day, to the full.

ENJOY LIFE by Artur Rubinstein from "Make No Conditions" by Artur Rubinstein. Reprinted with permission of The Macmillan Publishing Co., Inc. from IN MY OPINION: THE SEVENTEEN BOOK OF VERY IMPORTANT PERSONS by SEVENTEEN Magazine. (Copyright © 1966 by Triangle Communications, Inc.)

During my long life I have learned one lesson: that the most important thing is to realize why one is alive—and I think it is not only to build bridges or tall buildings or make money, but to do something truly important, to do something for humanity. To bring joy, hope, to make life richer for the spirit because you have been alive, that is the most important thing.

To me the world is divided into two kinds of people: those who are conscious and those who are unconscious. To me there is no difference among men when it comes to their color, their race, their religion; they are all equal. Only the degree of their awareness of the world they live in, of the joy and the pleasure of living, of the need of sharing that awareness with others and bringing it to their fellowmen . . . is a measure of this difference.

LESSON in FAITH

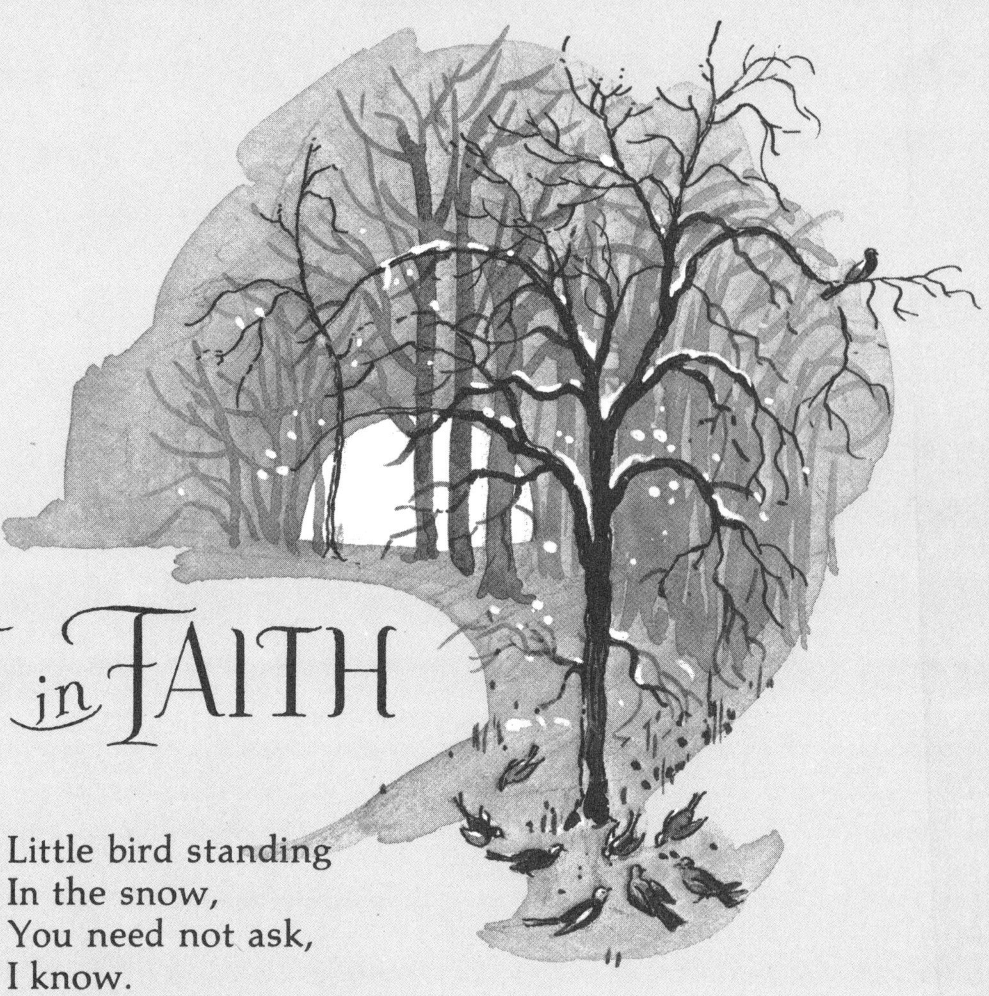

Little bird standing
In the snow,
You need not ask,
I know.

Your presence speaks
Quietly
Of faith
As it should be.

I feel the thrill
That in the still
Cold morning
You chose me.

Mary Wheeler Edgerton

Painting opposite
A LITTLE SAMARITAN
Photo, Picture Archives

Stone Soup

Marcia Brown

Three soldiers trudged down a road in a strange country. They were on their way home from the wars. Besides being tired, they were hungry. In fact, they had eaten nothing for two days.

"How I would like a good dinner tonight," said the first. "And a bed to sleep in," said the second. "But all that is impossible," said the third. "We must march on."

On they marched. Suddenly, ahead of them they saw the lights of a village. "Maybe we'll find a bite to eat there," said the first. "And a loft to sleep in," said the second. "No harm in asking," said the third.

Now the peasants of that place feared strangers. When they heard that three soldiers were coming down the road, they talked among themselves.

"Here come three soldiers. Soldiers are always hungry. But we have little enough for ourselves." And they hurried to hide their food. They pushed sacks of barley under the hay in the lofts. They lowered buckets of milk down the wells. They spread old quilts over the carrot bins. They hid their cabbages and potatoes under the beds. They hung their meat in the cellars. They hid all they had to eat. Then—they waited.

The soldiers stopped first at the house of Paul and Francoise. "Good evening to you," they said. "Could you spare a bit of food for three hungry solders?" "We have had no food for ourselves for three days," said Paul. Francoise made a sad face. "It has been a poor harvest."

The three soldiers went on to the house of Albert and Louise. "Could you spare a bit of food? And have you some corner where we could sleep for the night?" "Oh no," said Albert. "We gave all we could spare to soldiers who came before you." "Our beds are full," said Louise.

At Vincent and Marie's the answer was the same. It had been a poor harvest and all the grain must be kept for seed.

So it went all through the village. Not a peasant had any food to give away. They all had good reasons. One family had used the grain for feed. Another had an old sick father to care for. All had too many mouths to fill. The villagers stood in the street and sighed. They looked as hungry as they could.

The three soldiers talked together. Then the first soldier called out, "Good people!" The peasants drew near. "We are three hungry soldiers in a strange land. We have asked you for food, and you have no food. Well then, we'll have to make stone soup."

The peasants stared. Stone soup? That would be something to know about.

"First we'll need a large iron pot," the soldiers said. The peasants brought the largest pot they could find. How else to cook enough? "That's none too large," said the soldiers. "But it will do. And now, water to fill it and a fire to heat it." It took many buckets of water to fill the pot. A fire was built on the village square and the pot was set to boil.

"And now, if you please, three round, smooth stones." Those were easy enough to find. The peasants' eyes grew round as they watched the soldiers drop the stones into the pot.

"Any soup needs salt and pepper," said the soldiers, as they began to stir. Children ran to fetch salt and pepper.

"Stones like these generally make good soup. But oh, if there were carrots, it would be much better." "Why, I think I have a carrot or two," said Francoise, and off she ran. She came back with her apron full of carrots from the bin beneath the red quilt.

"A good stone soup should have cabbage," said the soldiers as they sliced the carrots into the pot. "But no use asking for what you don't have." "I think I could find a cabbage somewhere," said Marie, and she hurried home. Back she came with three cabbages from the cupboard under the bed.

"If we only had a bit of beef and a few potatoes, this soup would be good enough for a rich man's table." The peasants thought that over. They remembered their potatoes and the sides of beef hanging in the cellars.

They ran to fetch them. A rich man's soup—and all from a few stones. It seemed like magic!

"Ah," sighed the soldiers as they stirred in the beef and potatoes, "if we only had a little barley and a cup of milk! This soup would be fit for the king himself. Indeed he asked for just such a soup when last he dined with us." The peasants looked at each other. The soldiers had entertained the king! Well! "But—no use asking for what you don't have," the soldiers sighed. The peasants brought their barley from the lofts, they brought their milk from the wells. The soldiers stirred the barley and milk into the steaming broth while the peasants stared.

At last the soup was ready. "All of you shall taste," the soldiers said. "But first a table must be set." Great tables were placed in the square. And all around were lighted torches.

Such a soup! How good it smelled! Truly fit for a king. But then the peasants asked themselves, "Would not such a soup require bread—and a roast—and cider?" Soon a banquet was spread and everyone sat down to eat. Never had there been such a feast. Never had the peasants tasted such soup. And fancy, made from stones!

They ate and drank and ate and drank. And after that they danced. They danced and sang far into the night. At last they were tired. Then the three soldiers asked, "Is there not a loft where we could sleep?" "Let three such wise and splendid gentlemen sleep in a loft? Indeed! They must have the best beds in the village." So the first soldier slept in the priest's house. The second soldier slept in the baker's house. And the third soldier slept in the mayor's house.

In the morning the whole village gathered in the square to give them a send-off. "Many thanks for what you have taught us," the peasants said to the soldiers. "We shall never go hungry, now that we know how to make soup from stones." "Oh, it's all in knowing how," said the soldiers, and off they went down the road.

"Such men don't grow on every bush."

Youth and the Snow

Georgia B. Adams

I love to watch the little ones
  Enjoying winter's snow;
They frolic in the midst of it
  With faces all aglow.

Some have their shovels; others choose
  To build a snowman there,
Or maybe have a snowball fight
  Which everyone can share.

They laugh and sprint, yes, youth but knows
  The joy of simple things.
It takes me back to childhood days;
  Oh, how the memory clings!

Just watch them as they laugh and shout,
  See how their faces glow!
Just watch them rollick, frolic in
  The newly fallen snow!

Peaceful
Countryside

The countryside is peaceful now
Beneath its cape of snow.
The snow and February! What
    A beauty it bestows!

The snow-capped fences punctuate
The sprawling, nubbled fields.
I thrill to see the scenery
    The hand of winter wields!

There go the rabbit tracks in spurts;
The chattering squirrel I see
Darting among the apple trees—
    There's none as quick as he!

The farmhouses are nestled neath
Thick comforters of snow.
The snow and February! What
    A beauty it bestows!

Georgia B. Adams

To a friend's house
the road is never long.
Dutch Proverb

To An Old
Friend's House

It's never far to an old friend's house,
    And the way is smooth and fine;
The path bears many a telltale mark
    Of footprints . . . his and mine.

The day is always bright and fair
    When I, on a friend would call,
Who's been a friend in time and stress
    And stood by through it all.

Each hill and vale and winding curve,
    Its youthful fancies lend,
And miles are short when I go forth
    To the house of an old, old friend.

Though skies are drear and clouds hang low
    And the outlook drab and gray,
There's a radiant glow at an old friend's house
    That drives the gloom away.

Time never drags at an old friend's house
    And the hours are filled with joy;
He pictures me and I picture him
    As a carefree laughing boy.

Old faces beam with wrinkled smiles,
    And the long years brightly blend
In a wealth of treasured memories—
    At the house of an old, old friend!

Adam N. Reiter

Photograph opposite
Three Lions, Inc.

GRANDMA'S QUILT

My grandma has a crazy quilt; but it's a story quilt to me,
For every piece that's in it has its history.

She starts up in the corner and she goes from left to right;
She tells me each one's story when I stay with her at night.

A fuzzy piece of cashmere she wore to her first ball;
That's where she met my grandpa, so proud, erect and tall.

That shiny square of satin was her own wedding dress,
The floral print beside it belonged to sister Bess.

The silky striped material was a piece of grandpa's tie,
The one just to the right of it belonged to Uncle Sy.

There is one she calls her party dress she said was trimmed with lace,
And it brings happy memories and smiles to Grandma's face.

A pale pink piece of taffeta with blue forget-me-nots
Belonged to my own mother when she was just a tot.

These funny little pieces that look so strange to me,
All mean love and friendship in Grandma's memories.

Some are dresses of her friends who are gone she knows not where;
Some bring a smile and some a tear as she tells each story there.

She tells me of the pretty things her mother used to wear,
Of tiny waists and full, hooped skirts and ribbons in their hair.

Her faded eyes grow wistful, an arm slips round my waist;
And as she draws me to her, a tear rolls down her face.

And then it's time to go to bed; I help her climb the stairs.
She tucks me in the story quilt and hears my bedtime prayers.

I hope some day, when I grow old, this quilt belongs to me;
And I'll unfold it proudly and tell its history.

Bernice V. Roberts

Front Row . . . Center Aisle

Come to one of those magic places,
Away from the cold and wind-chilled faces,
Where art is scarce and fame is fleeting;
You'll be assured of perfect seating.
An interesting, casual place to go,
 The children are staging a puppet show.

Come, transformed by separate worlds,
Where evil lurks and girls have curls,
Where whistling sound and eerie light
Create a scene of sheer delight,
A splash of red, a golden glow,
 The children are staging a puppet show.

Come for a moment, drift away
Where things unusual hold full sway.
Back when knighthood was in flower
And damsels dwelt in rose-topped bower,
Dragons were made of calico;
 The children are staging a puppet show.

Come where friendships never end,
Evil wears a sneaky grin,
Right must triumph over wrong,
Weakness, helped by faith, grows strong.
These are truths the world should know;
 The children are staging a puppet show.

Come where the present meets the past,
Where signs and wonders move the cast
To lands that childhood sets apart.
Their simple beauty warms the heart.
Beyond the meadow deep with snow,
 The children are staging a puppet show.

Sara Bren

February

Here comes February, a little girl with her first valentine, a red bow in her wind-blown hair, a kiss waiting on her lips, a tantrum just back of her laughter. She is young as a kitten, changeable as the wind, and into everything. She can sulk, she can beam, she changes from one minute to the next. February is a phase, a short phase at that, and she has to be lived with.

February can't be taken seriously too long at a time. It starts with Groundhog Day, which is neither omen nor portent, but only superstition, and it ends, often as not, in a flurry of snow. It is sleet and snow and ice and cold, and now and then it is waxing sunshine and tantalizing thaw and promise. February is soup and mittens, and it is a shirt-sleeve day that demands an overcoat before sundown. It is forsythia buds opening in the house and skid chains clanking on the highway. February is sunrise at 6:30 for the first time since November.

February is a gardener pruning his grape vines today and shoveling a two-foot drift off the front walk tomorrow morning. It is a farmer wondering this week if his hay will last the Winter, and next week wondering if he should start plowing. It is tiny, tight catkins on the alder in the swamp and skunk cabbage thrusting a green sheath up through the ice. February is the tag end of Winter—we hope. But in our hearts we know it isn't Spring, not by several weeks and at least a dozen degrees.

There's no evidence to support it in the dictionaries, but some say that February's name comes from an ancient and forgotten word meaning "a time that tries the patience."

Hal Borland

The Brook

The tireless brook through winter's snows
Pursues its course and onward goes
O'er twig and stone, now left, now right,
It winds its way by day and night
As if in haste to find the chance
To join the ocean's vast expanse.

The trees that grace its ragged bank
Like sentinels on either flank
Stand staunch and steadfast through the years,
Dispelling winter's snow-bound fears,
And giving forth the promise true
That soon the summer will be due.

The house that dots the distant hill
Now feels the winter's icy chill,
But soon the warming sun will come
And cause the snow to swiftly run
To join the rushing brook in glee
That now its action will be free.

How like the brook we humans are,
We ever seek that goal afar
Where we shall merge our lives at last
In seas whose depths engulf the past,
Whose shores bid us our struggles cease
And live henceforth in perfect peace.

George Z. Keller

Photograph opposite
Mt. Vernon, Wisconsin
Ken Dequaine

February is the short month, according to the calendar. In our valley it is often called the hardest month. This is partly because we have had enough winter, and even the most beautiful snowfall has lost its excitement. The wind blows colder and has a wild melancholy wail. The experts say that the air is actually denser than in summer, so there is more force in that wind. All I know is that the old farmhouse seems drafty, and I stuff paper toweling along the sills in my bedroom.

The furnace huffs along, resting only occasionally, and it is now a comforting sound instead of a nuisance. My bedroom is directly over the part of the cellar where the furnace is located, and in December, I sometimes complain about the noise; but in February, I am glad to hear it in the middle of the night as the lonely wind cries.

The fire burns steadily on the hearth in the keeping room, not only because its cheerful warmth is heartwarming and good for toasting chilled toes but because it also keeps the cold air from swooping down the great chimney. And then the crackle of the logs is such a good sound! The woodpile, which is right outside the keeping-room windows, has now diminished so that it no longer reaches to the windowsills, but there is plenty left to last through April—and possibly May and June.

But February is never monotonous. There comes a day when the air seems lighter and warmer and the icicles on the well house melt and the February thaw has come. It is a promise that winter is in the final phase and nature is once more following her cycle toward spring. And when I look out of my window I see a dark streak flowing down the big maple as the sap rises once more. The time varies from year to year, but it is always in February that that first real sign of spring to come is visible.

If the thaw lasts long enough, I can hear the brook running down the hill to the pond, carrying ice lace to the water below. It will freeze quiet again, but it has that sense of release to come.

The birds are hungrier than ever. They empty the bird feeders twice daily. Seeds and berries are scarce. The squirrels must have mislaid their nuts, for they swarm over the feeders. The barn cats from all over the neighborhood wrench the suet from the suet cage in hunks. And I fill a big bowl of kibbles for them daily as well. I can see why some Indians called this the Hunger Moon.

Social life in the valley is restricted now to a minimum. Neighbors preface invitations for supper with "If the roads are bad or there is another ice storm, don't try to come out." Jean Lovdal manages to have something that will keep, and my favorite is her spareribs. I will try to get to the Lovdals even if I skid all the way, so it is fortunate they live nearby.

This recipe calls for 4 pounds spareribs, cracked through the middle and cut in serving pieces and broiled until brown. Drain off the fat. Dissolve 2 bouillon cubes in 1½ cups boiling water, and add ¼ cup hot catsup, 3 tablespoons Worcestershire sauce, 1 tablespoon cider vinegar, dash of cayenne, ½ teaspoon celery salt, 3 whole cloves, 3 whole allspice, ½ bay leaf, and 1 medium-size onion, peeled and sliced. Pour this over the ribs, cover with foil, and bake in a hot oven (400°) until tender—about 2 hours. Jean serves this with chunks of French bread to dunk in the sauce and a green salad, and nothing could be more delicious.

Gladys Taber

River Journey

The snow is melting all around
   with all its water rushing down
      to join with others on the land
         to form the rivers close at hand.

The sound of water spilling free
   flows through the mountains and the trees
      and rushing, twisting, roaring by,
         at times, will slow to breathe a sigh.

Then on again to form the falls
   whose vision from below enthralls,
      and pools of blue and green abound
         where waiting rainbow trout are found.

This all leads down to flattened land,
   across the plains and through the sand,
      and on it flows so wild and free
         to end its journey at the sea.

Fred Dougherty

Photograph opposite
Alpha Photo Associates, Inc.

Overleaf photograph
Freelance Photographers Guild

Spring Water

There is a little spring beside the lane
Whose waters are as clear as crystal glass,
That bubbles up into a little pool,
Rock rimmed and cold where moving shadows pass
Across its face, like figures on a screen,
Where tangled grass and weeping willows lean.

It tastes of shale and twigs and sodden leaves
The odors of the earth, green moss and peat,
The roots of quiet trees and rotting logs,
The crumbling bank where cowslips wash their feet
And tiny minnows dart with lightning speed
Among the roots where wild ducks come to feed.

And so the little spring of water holds
The very core and essence of the earth.
The taste of melted snow and sleet and rain,
Clover and sorrel root, the trembling mirth
Of birds who roost amid the tree tops high
And breathe the wholesome fragrance of the sky.

Edna Jaques

When Dreams Come True

When dreams come true, as your dreams have
And life is kind and sweet,
When everything is right, it seems
To make your world complete.
How very little else you need,
Each day is filled with bliss
When you've a love to call your own,
·A tender sweetheart's kiss.

When dreams come true for special friends
We like to have a share,
To let them know in some small way
How very much we care.
How much we prize their happiness
And though words might be few,
My heart is filled with tender thoughts
I'd like to share with you.

When dreams come true, though time may pass
However long it's been,
The gladness of that precious day
Can always live again.
And time cannot erase the smiles
The mem'ries you have known;
It still was only yesterday
That love became your own.

When dreams can live as your dreams have
Through each new passing year,
To add more happiness and joy,
To grow more sweet and dear.
Just two in love, and sweethearts still
In everything you do,
Because true love lives in your hearts
And blesses dreams come true.

Garnett Ann Schultz

Photograph opposite
Robert Cushman Hayes

My Treasured Valentine

Fashioned of most bewitching things
    As hearts and arrows, bows and strings,
Gay, gallant youths with maidens fair
    Of coral lips and powdered hair,
Baby's breath and roses twine
    To guard my treasured Valentine.

'Tis laid most carefully away
    With other wealth in sweet sachet,
And though 'tis in old-fashioned dress
    Its tender words of love express
The same dear thought that knows not time
    Of "Will you be my Valentine?"

Esther Cushman Randall

Photograph opposite
Gerald Koser

The ABC's of Friendship

Alice Leedy Mason

The absolute zenith— beginnings and ends—
A to Z thoughts on friendship and friends.

A is that amiable and affable ally,
An associate who loves you and doesn't ask why.

B means you're blessed with the brightest and best,
Beyond your belief when brought to the test.

C is a charming companion who cares,
Who champions your interests, includes you in prayers.

D means dynamic, delightful and dear.
A down-to-earth slayer of dragons of fear.

E stands for excellent, eager to cope;
Effectively employing the essence of hope.

F is for friendship, filled from the start
With firm unforgettable feelings of heart.

G is the greatest— that gift most admired—
Guardian of good things, sought and desired.

H is for happiness, the heavenly kind.
The honest exchange of heart and of mind.

I shows that interests, imaginative displays,
Are like your own image in so many ways.

J is that jewel of judgment so keen,
Acknowledged by glances exchanged on the scene.

K shows the keeper of confidence cares
And never discloses your personal affairs.

L is for laughter like birds in free flight,
And love so uplifting it makes the heart light.

M means the magic of moment and place,
Mutual memories that time can't erase.

N never needs a nobler name
Than neighbor— nearby and ever the same.

O stands for one with objectives to lend
And open-eyed faith in the worth of a friend.

P is that partner whose patience and praise
Provide prayerful guidance for impossible days.

Q means a quiet and thoughtful reply
When the quest is for something on which to rely.

R means remarkable, ready to stand,
Realistic, reliable— a sturdy right hand.

S stands for special, a sensitive soul,
Who loves you in spite of opinions you hold.

T is some thoughtful sweet-treat or bouquet
That suddenly arrives on the world's toughest day.

U 's the unusual, unforgettable thing.
The unconquerable strength that friendship can bring.

V is that starry-eyed vision achieved
By the valiant persuasion of one who believed.

W 's the wonderful, warm-hearted one
Who comforts in sorrow and joins you in fun.

X is Xpression, Xcitement, Xpert—
An Xperience that lessens the chances that hurt.

Y is for YOU and for years that can yield
The true depth of friendship that time can reveal.

Z is for Zest! Be someone who shares.
To have a friend is to be one who cares.
Love is the answer that ties the loose ends.

A to Z thoughts on friendship and friends.

A Loving Family

There's nothing like a family
To set a heart aglow;
A mom and dad and little ones,
So much a joy to know,
A peaceful home where laughter lives
And children there abide.
Oh, nothing else can ever match
The love that lives inside.

There's nothing like a family
Just at the close of day,
The evening meal, then happy hours,
And little hearts that pray,
A fireside bright, the books and games;
It seems that angels keep
A loving vigil round the beds
Where precious children sleep.

Somehow it seems that love doth dwell
In understanding souls,
While hurts and problems disappear
And each would seek his goal;
Whatever else, it matters not
While minds are bright and free,
And God is ever present in
A loving family.

Garnett Ann Schultz

Photograph opposite
Alpha Photo Associates, Inc.

A Tribute to Lincoln

*The better part
of one's life consists of his friendships.*

Abraham Lincoln

A man of great ability, pure patriotism, unselfish nature, full of forgiveness to his enemies, bearing malice toward none, he proved to be the man above all others for the struggle through which the nation had to pass to place itself among the greatest in the family of nations. His fame will grow brighter as time passes and his great, great work is better understood.

Ulysses S. Grant

From *Lincoln, the Man of the People*

The color of the ground was in him, the red earth,
The smack and tang of elemental things:
The rectitude and patience of the cliff,
The good-will of the rain that loves all leaves,
The friendly welcome of the wayside well,
The courage of the bird that dares the sea,
The gladness of the wind that shakes the corn,
The pity of the snow that hides all scars,
The secrecy of streams that make their way
Under the mountain to the rifted rock,
The tolerance and equity of light
That gives as freely to the shrinking flower
As to the great oak flaring to the wind—
To the grave's low hill as to the Matterhorn
That shoulders out the sky.

So came the Captain with the mighty heart;
And when the judgment thunders split the house,
Wrenching the rafters from their ancient rest,
He held the ridgepole up, and spiked again
The rafters of the Home. He held his place—
Held the long purpose like a growing tree—
Held on through blame and faltered not at praise—
Towering in calm rough-hewn sublimity.
And when he fell in whirlwind, he went down
As when a lordly cedar, green with boughs,
Goes down with a great shout upon the hills,
And leaves a lonesome place against the sky.

Edwin Markham

A slender acquaintance with the world
must convince every man that actions, not words,
are the true criterion of the attachment of friends;
and that the most liberal profession of good-will
is very far from being the surest mark of it.

George Washington

The Inscription at Mount Vernon

Washington, the brave, the wise, the good,
Supreme in war, in council, and in peace,
Valiant without ambition, discreet without fear,
Confident without presumption.
In disaster, calm; in success, moderate;
In all, himself.

> The hero, the patriot, the Christian.
> The father of nations, the friend of mankind,
> Who, when he had won all, renounced all,
> And sought in the bosom of his family
> And of nature, retirement,
> And in the hope of religion, immortality.

First in War, First in Peace

First in war, first in peace, and first in the hearts of his countrymen, he was second to none in the humble and endearing scenes of private life. Pious, just, humane, temperate and sincere; uniform, dignified and commanding, his example was as edifying to all around him, as were the effects of that example lasting.

Henry Lee

A PRESIDENT REMEMBERS

Dwight D. Eisenhower

Mother and Father maintained a genuine partnership in raising their six sons. Father was a breadwinner, Supreme Court, and Lord High Executioner. Mother was tutor and manager of our household. Their partnership was ideal. This may sound unbelievable, and only recollected in tranquillity, but I never heard a cross word pass between them. Never did I hear them disagree on a value judgment in family, social, or economic affairs—not that there weren't sufficient causes. I never had any indication that they were annoyed with each other. Before their children, they were not demonstrative in their love for each other, but a quiet, mutual devotion permeated in our home. This had its lasting effect on all the boys.

Normally, Father worked six days a week. He usually left the house about 6:30 and came home about 5:00. Family life revolved around him. School, chores, meals, and all other activities— winter and summer—had to be adjusted to meet his requirements. His work was hard and the pay was meager. . . .

My mother's household problems were, I realize now, monumental. The least of them was to provide comfortable beds for six boys in three rooms. She skillfully assigned us to beds in such a pattern as to minimize the incidence of nightly fights. She rotated our duties; helping with the cooking, dishwashing, laundry (she never had reason to miss the assistance usually provided by daughters); pruning the orchard, harvesting the fruit and storing it for winter; hoeing the corn and weeding the vegetable garden; putting up the hay in our immense barn; feeding the chickens and milking the cow. By rotating chores weekly, each son learned all the responsibilities of running the house and none felt discriminated against. The total task of making life happy and meaningful for a family of eight took insight, imagination, and managerial skill.

Mother rarely resorted to corporal punishment and when she did it was a slap on the hand with a ruler or anything handy and lightweight. Instead, she deeply believed in self-discipline and she preached it constantly. According to her, each of us should behave properly not because of the fear of punishment but because it was the right thing to do. Such a philosophy was a trifle idealistic for a platoon of growing boys but in later years we came to understand her ideas better.

Mother took care of minor infractions during the day but anything serious was passed along to Father for settlement. With his family of hearty, active boys, I'm sure that strict discipline was necessary for survival. He certainly was never one for spoiling any child by sparing the rod. If the evidence showed that the culprit had offended deliberately, the application of stick to skin was a routine affair.

Father had quick judicial instincts. Mother had, like a psychologist, insight into the fact that each son was a unique personality and she adapted her methods to each. . . .

Both parents were against quarreling and fighting. They deplored bad manners. I did discover one day that my father was far from being a turn-the-other-cheek type. He arrived home early one afternoon as I came in from the school grounds on the run, chased by a belligerent boy of about my own size. Seeing this, my father called: "Why do you let that boy run you around like that?"

Instantly I shouted back, "Because if I fight him, you'll give me a whipping, whether I win or lose!"

"Chase that boy out of here."

This was enough for me. I turned around and it was the suddenness of my counterattack, rather than any fighting prowess that startled my tormentor, who took off at a rapid pace. I, being faster, was more than overjoyed when I caught him, threw him down to the ground, and voiced threats of violence. He seemed to take these most seriously. In fact, I promised to give him a thrashing every day unless he let me alone. I was rapidly learning that domination of others in this world often comes or is sought through bluff. But it took me some years to learn that pounding from an opponent is not to be dreaded as much as constantly living in fear of another. . . .

Usually, Father was quiet and reserved. Mother was by far the greatest personal influence in our lives. She spent many hours a day with us, while Father's time with us was largely at supper and in the evening. In the end, his desire for his sons' education was fulfilled by four of them. . . . Years later, when Arthur was an authority on grain marketing finance and banking, Edgar a successful lawyer and director of industrial companies,

Earl a radio station owner and public relations director of the community newspaper, Milton President of Johns Hopkins University, and I first administration Republican President, friends often asked why there had not been a black sheep in the family.

I have often thought about this. The answer lies, I think in the fact that our family life was free from parental quarreling and filled with genuine, if not demonstrated love. I never knew anyone from a divorced family until I went to West Point. Responsibility was a part of maturing. Concern for others was natural in our small community. And ambition without arrogance was quietly instilled in us by both parents. Part of that ambition was self-dependence. My mother could recite from memory long passages of the Bible (family tradition has it that she once won first prize in her church, as a child in Virginia, by memorizing 1365 verses in a six-month period). But these were not her only admonitions. Whenever any of us expressed a wish for something that seemed far beyond our reach, my mother often said, "Sink or swim," or "Survive or perish."

Friends Are Like Flowers

Friends are like flowers. I have found them so:
The hardy staunch perennials that grow
Year after year, are like some friends I know.

Some must be nursed with frequent trowel and spade,
And sheltered from the sun or too much shade,
For fear their frail and clinging bloom may fade,

One need not cultivate them with great care,
They only need the sun, and wind, and air
Of trust and love, and they are always there.

Friends are like flowers. I would be a friend
Whose blossomings no hand need ever tend:
A perennial on whom hearts can depend.

Grace Noll Crowell

"Friends Are Like Flowers" from POEMS OF INSPIRATION AND COURAGE by
Grace Noll Crowell. Copyright 1942 by Harper & Row, Publishers, Inc.; renewed 1970
by Reid Crowell. Reprinted by permission of the publisher.

Photograph opposite
Gerald Koser

To My Dear Friend Haydn

February 9 of this year marks the 223rd anniversary
of the birth of one of the world's most gifted musical geniuses.
Although the life of Wolfgang Amadeus Mozart
ended a short thirty-five years after his birth,
his compositions brought profound stylistic changes
to the music of his time,
changes that are now considered paramount contributions.
At three, Mozart played harpsichord, violin and organ;
at five, he began to compose.
Unfortunately, the brilliance of this child prodigy
went largely unrecognized.
His music was derogated as ponderous and modernistic.
Because of this lack of acceptance and recognition,
Mozart lost, for a time, his ability to produce.
Joseph Haydn was the only contemporary musician
to recognize the value of Mozart's genius.
At a time when Mozart needed support and guidance,
Haydn's paternal friendship proved as valuable
as his musical example.

Excerpt from: *Mozart*
— *A Pictorial Biography*

Erich Valentin

[*In Vienna, at Mozart's house near St. Stephan's, parties were often attended by many illustrious guests, including, of course, Mozart's contemporaries in the field of music.*]

One of these guests, who came as a friend and remained a friend throughout his life, was Joseph Haydn. The association between Haydn and Mozart can only be compared with the friendship between Goethe and Schiller. Haydn, considerably older than Mozart, played the role of advisor, teacher, and father confessor. It is a tribute to the greatness of both that the younger had no reservations about benefiting from the experience of the elder, and that the elder, this is particularly unusual, was no less delighted to be a "pupil" of the younger. In 1781, with his Russian Quartets, Joseph Haydn had succeeded in attaining the style which is now called "classical." Mozart, gripped by these works, took up the idea and developed it further in a series of six quartets which he completed in 1785 and dedicated to Haydn. The actual phraseology of the dedication he appended to these "fruits of a long and difficult period of work" are an expression of a deeply felt and sensitive friendship. The moving dedication begs Haydn to become the "Father, Guide, and Friend" of "my six sons." Personally, too, it must have had significance. Haydn acknowledged it, for his part, when he dedicated various pieces of his own later works to Wolfgang Amadeus Mozart.

What a Friend We Have in Jesus

JOSEPH SCRIVEN   CHARLES C. CONVERSE

1. What a Friend we have in Je-sus,   All our sins and griefs to bear!
2. Have we tri-als and temp-ta-tions?   Is there trou-ble an-y-where?
3. Are we weak and heav-y-la-den,   Cum-bered with a load of care?

What a priv-i-lege to car-ry   Ev-'ry-thing to God in pray'r!
We should nev-er be dis-cour-aged,   Take it to the Lord in pray'r!
Pre-cious Sav-ior, still our ref-uge,   Take it to the Lord in pray'r!

O what peace we oft-en for-feit,   O what need-less pain we bear,
Can we find a friend so faith-ful   Who will all our sor-rows share?
Do thy friends de-spise, for-sake thee?   Take it to the Lord in pray'r;

All be-cause we do not car-ry   Ev-'ry-thing to God in pray'r!
Je-sus knows our ev-'ry weak-ness,   Take it to the Lord in pray'r.
In His arms He'll take and shield thee,   Thou wilt find a sol-ace there.

Joseph Scriven led a very quiet, helpful life in Port Hope, Canada. He tried to be a friend to everyone in need and was always willing to work hard for those less fortunate than himself. Few persons knew he could write poetry until a friend found the words to this hymn one day and asked him about them. Although he replied "They were written to comfort my mother at one time. I never intended anyone else to see them," we are glad he was willing to let them be published so others might also gain comfort and help from them.

The Children's Hour

A whisper, and then a silence:
  Yet I know by their merry eyes
They are plotting and planning together
  To take me by surprise.

A sudden rush from the stairway,
  A sudden raid from the hall!
By three doors left unguarded
  They enter my castle wall!

They climb up into my turret
  O'er the arms and back of my chair;
If I try to escape, they surround me;
  They seem to be everywhere.

They almost devour me with kisses,
  Their arms about me entwine
Till I think of the Bishop of Bingen
  In his Mouse-Tower on the Rhine!

Do you think, O blue-eyed banditti,
  Because you have scaled the wall,
Such an old mustache as I am
  Is not a match for you all?

I have you fast in my fortress,
  And will not let you depart,
But put you down into the dungeon
  In the round-tower of my heart.

And there will I keep you forever,
  Yes, forever and a day,
Till the walls shall crumble to ruin,
  And moulder in dust away!

Between the dark and the daylight,
  When the night is beginning to lower,
Comes a pause in the day's occupations
  That is known as the Children's Hour.

I hear in the chamber above me
  The patter of little feet,
The sound of a door that is opened
  And voices soft and sweet.

From my study I see in the lamplight,
  Descending the broad hall stair,
Grave Alice and laughing Allegra,
  And Edith with golden hair.

Henry Wadsworth Longfellow

A Welcomed Peace

Nothing could be lovelier
  Than the glow of setting sun,
As the weary earth slips into sleep
When the end of day has come.

A rich man's finest treasures
  Could never match its worth,
For a sunset is our tiny part
  Of Heaven here on earth.

All trouble seems to disappear
  For with it sunset brings
A gentle breath of welcomed peace
  To every living thing.

Resting is His weary world
  From a day's long journey trod,
And the warmth of a glowing sunset
  Is a kiss goodnight from God.

Sharon Mellon

At Sunset

When the sun sinks low on the western world
  In a blaze of blue and gold,
And the trees stand dark against the sky
  As the shades of night unfold,
Then I give my day to the Lord again,
  All that it was is my gift,
And then rest assured that His will be done
  And my heart with joy shall lift.

Mildred Spires Jacobs

Photograph opposite
Freedom, New Hampshire
Fred Sieb

A Boy and His Dog

A boy and his dog make a glorious pair;
No better friendship is found anywhere,
For they talk, and they walk, and they run, and they play,
And they have their deep secrets for many a day;
And that boy has a comrade who thinks and who feels,
Who walks down the road with a dog at his heels.

He may go where he will and his dog will be there,
May revel in mud and his dog will not care;
Faithful he'll stay for the highest command
And bark with delight at the touch of his hand;
Oh, he owns a treasure which nobody steals,
Who walks down the road with a dog at his heels.

No other can lure him away from his side;
He's proof against riches and station and pride;
Fine dress does not charm him, and flattery's breath
Is lost on the dog, for he's faithful to death;
He sees the great soul which the body conceals—
Oh, it's great to be young with a dog at your heels!

Edgar A. Guest

Magic Time

A magic time when wanderlust
Fills the mind and heart;
A magic time when blossoms blow
And winter snows depart;

A magic time when friend to friend
Send greetings far and near;
And now this is the magic time
To greet all friends so dear.

Eleanor Fiock

See that you never despise any of these young ones,
for I tell you that their angels are continually in the presence
of my Father in heaven.

Matt. 18:10

I Am Young

I am young.
I'd like to tell you about my strong sense of reaching
out, of breaking away from yesterday with its do's and
don'ts; of greeting today and living it—really living it—and
giving a grateful welcome to tomorrow. Together we can
learn to appreciate again the freshness of life, the cool, sweet
newnesses perhaps now dimmed in yours. So many of the
things I think about seem to surge from down deep inside me.
I am young.
What I need from you is your quiet understanding that
will web me in your wisdom subtly. I need your presence,
denied me by modern housing and care facilities. I need
to grow toward you and you toward me.
I am young.
I need your example to support me much
more than your advice. I need your patience, your
tolerance, your sense of humor as you recall what
it was to be inexperienced and sometimes foolish.
I am young.
I hope our concern to help, teach, or care for each
other will not cancel out our own offerings. I need you to
listen to what I dream, to what I feel; and to let me know you
treasure my sharing.
We are young,
For how can intermittent growth be turned off? Society often says kids and the
elderly aren't important, that only "productive" adults signify—but I need your help; we
need each other. Let me do for you and you for me.
I am young.
My quest for a life-force for the maker of this wondrous world builds slowly. I feel it will take
ages before I know who it really is and learn to respond comfortably. Will you speak to me of your search, of
your prayer?

Kevin Robertson, SSSF

Ask your elders.
Let them enlighten you.
                Deut. 32:7

I Am Old

I am old.

I invite you to understand my new sense of letting go as my call to say good-bye to yesterday and to welcome today and tomorrow with all the changes that they bring into my life. I can help you learn to "let go" by being reminder to you that you are not in full control; that certain circumstances of your life which you may not think about very often or which you do not wish to think about are real, and the best way to meet these is from a place of inner freedom deep within yourself.

I am old.

What I need from you is not your training in how to be with me, not the kind of specialization that society might say you need. What I need is your simple, but profound presence to me—and mine to you. Then, both of us will keep growing, and you and I will really meet.

I am old.

I may need your arm to support me, but much more—I need your gentle touch that says you care. I am not weak and you strong. We are both complex yet fragile human beings.

I am old.

I hope your readiness and your real concern to teach or to administer or to care for me will not prevent you from receiving what I have to offer you. I need you simply to soak in what I have to give you, and to let me know that you cherish it as gift.

I am old.

For my continued growing, I cannot be segregated. I need you to help me make one-to-one contact with young people. I need and want the comfort and consolation of seeing my life continued in them, somehow, and they need and deserve my experience and my stories and my insights.

I am old.

My search for God, my journey to Him has lasted long, long years—and it's not yet over. But I can tell you who He is to me—and of the prayers I love. And it would be such gift to me to hear you talk of Him—and your search—and your prayer.

Lauretta Mather, SSSF

On the following six pages,
we are presenting a selection
from Friendly Ideals 1947.

FRIENDLY
ideals

Friendly Street –

By Mary Jean Shurtz

I followed a street that was wide, and led
Down a friendly way, where the folks, instead
Of thinking that they were always right,
Would admit that sometimes they were not . . . quite.
And all the folks on this friendly street
Had a cheery smile when we chanced to meet
They would say "hello" in a friendly tone,
And you cared for them like your very own.
There was not one person along the way
Who would mar the happiness of the day.
And it was a place where just friends meet,
This pleasant and wide old friendly street.

And those who lived there were the kind who say,
"Well, what if he did do a wrong today?
Last night, when the rest of you were asleep,
I heard him talk and I heard him weep;
And he knelt and prayed till dawn was aflame
And still the right answer never came—
Or perhaps it WAS right—who are we to say
That it was an error he made today?"
There's a side to that and a side to this—
Couldn't we be the ones who might really miss?
Oh, it was a pleasure to meet and greet
The folks who lived on this friendly street.

But the street I followed was in a dream;
I've found that, often, in life's great scheme
Where it's made of the folks we know
Who over the rough paths, and even, go,
When the going's rough, and we sometimes make
The turn that will end in a sad mistake,
There's a good side there if we care to find
That side, instead of being so unkind.
But the man who KNOWS he is always right
And the world is wrong—and there's no respite
For the man who has strayed; will never meet
You, and cheer you on, down this friendly street.

Oh, I'd hate to be, when life here is through,
The man who was certain that only he knew
The right side of every trial that came,
And that those he chose were the ones to blame.
For I'm certain God will have mercy there
For the man who erred; and—I hope—to spare
For the man who stands at the Judgment Seat
To explain why HIS was FRIENDLY STREET.

A Day of a Year Long Ago

By Al Langan

Oh, just give me a day of a year long ago
At a little school house huddled deep in the snow.
The teacher with pointer indicating the verb,
And the water can's hiss on the stove could be heard.

*The banging and clatter of the scuttle's black snout,
As the coal rattled in and the smoke billowed out,
The frost pictures melting, forming pools on the sills,
The hush and the beauty of snow covered hills.*

The explosion released at the noon recess hour
At the sound of the bell in the little square tower,
When nineteen young bodies were uncoiled with a roar
And laughing and yelling made a dash for the door.

*Then rolling and tumbling in the snow for a spell
Were recalled for their lunch by the clang of the bell;
'Mid rattling of paper and the fragrant spiced scent
Of pickles and apples, lunch and hour were soon spent.*

Then back to our lessons, for our teacher was firm,
Through geog'phy and hist'ry three more hours would we squirm;
The clock hands turned slowly, the hours creeping away
'Till at last rang the bell for the end of the day.

Amid jingle and crunch speeding down the hill road
Came the sleighs and the sleds for their wriggling young load,
And with shouted farewells through the quickening gloam
We bundled and covered for the gliding ride home.

The horses were eager and their mouths flecked with foam,
The trees flashed by quickly as we headed for home.
When we passed by their house, we dropped Jim and Lenore
And soon jumped from the sled at our own kitchen door.

Then 'round the big table for a fine winter treat,
From dome covered dishes for conserving the heat
Came such wealth of good things in which mother took pride
That our belts were stretched tight as we pushed chairs aside.

With a lingering look at the table now bare
We ran to the parlor to get curled in a chair
To study our lessons by the stove glowing red
Or play just a little, then upstairs to our bed.

And rest came so quickly, for our cares were so light
That soon the whole household was asleep for the night.
Yes, just give me a day of a year long ago,
Just a day from the days that are now running low.

Thank You, Friend...

I never came to you, my friend,
And went away without
Some new enrichment of the heart:
More faith and less of doubt,
More courage for the days ahead;
And often in great need
Coming to you, I went away
Comforted indeed.

How can I find the shining word,
The glowing phrase that tells
All that your love has meant to me,
All that your friendship spells?
There is no word, no phrase for you
On whom I so depend—
All I can say to you is this:
God bless you, precious friend.

By Grace Noll Crowell

Dear Subscriber:

Ideals is growing and our growth is in no small part due to your continued acceptance of our publications. As a direct result, we will be publishing two new issues which will be included in our upcoming one-year subscription program. New Ideals subscribers will now receive eight issues rather than the six issues we had previously offered.

The new subscriptions will be offered at $16.00 per subscription. There is, however, additional information which will pertain to our existing subscribers on the special insert included in this issue.

Our 1979 subscription program will begin with "Friendship Ideals" released in January of 1979. In addition to the six previously scheduled issues of Ideals, we will be offering a delightful spring-time release entitled "Mother's Day Ideals" scheduled for publication during March of 1979. In August of 1979 the colorful "Autumn Ideals," a salute to the beauty of the golden season and quite distinct from our "Thanksgiving Ideals," will also be published.

We trust you will be as thrilled with our new program as we are and we are looking forward to your continued patronage.

We thank you, our subscribers, for making this expansion possible through your past and continued support.

Sincerely,
The Editor

Statement of ownership, management and circulation (Required by 39 U.S.C., 3685), of IDEALS, published approximately every 6 weeks at Milwaukee, Wisconsin for September 1978. Publisher, Ideals Publishing Corporation; Editorial Director, James Kuse; Managing Editor, Ralph Luedtke; Owner, Harlequin Enterprises BV, Prinsengracht 778, Amsterdam, The Netherlands 1002. The known bondholders, mortgagees, and other security holders owning or holding 1 percent or more of total amount of bonds, mortgages or other securities are: None. Average no. copies each issue during preceding 12 months: Total no. copies printed (Net Press Run) 239,582. Paid circulation 70,127. Mail subscriptions 160,547. Total paid circulation 230,674. Free distribution 400. Total distribution 231,074. Single issue nearest to filing date: Total no. copies printed (Net Press Run) 199,378. Paid circulation 26,465. Other sales 164,280. Free distribution 400. Total distribution 191,145. I certify that the statements made by me above are correct and complete. William G. Gaspero, President/C.E.O.

Coming in Easter Ideals—

A special feature: "Empty Tomb, Full Heart" . . . biblical passages of the Easter story . . . Michelangelo's *Pieta* . . . Ideals Best-Loved Poet, Georgia B. Adams . . . Pages from the Past, Easter Ideals, 1947 . . . plus poetry and prose expressing the joy of Easter.

ACKNOWLEDGMENTS

PEACEFUL COUNTRYSIDE by Georgia B. Adams. From THE SILVER FLUTE AND OTHER POEMS by Georgia B. Adams. Copyright © 1968 by Georgia B. Adams. Published by Dorrance & Company. A BOY AND HIS DOG by Edgar A. Guest. Copyrighted. Used by permission of Reilly & Lee Co. FAITHFUL FRIEND; THE FRIENDLY TOUCH; FRIENDLY WORLD; I THANK MY FRIENDS . . . and REAL FOLKS by James J. Metcalfe. Copyrighted. Courtesy Field Enterprises, Inc.

Additional photo credits: Front cover, Freelance Photographers Guild. Inside front cover, Fred Sieb. Inside back cover, Robert Holland. Back cover, Hampfler Studios.